SAVING ANIMALS

SAVING MOUNTAIN
GORILLAS

by Lisa Bullard

T0014924

FOCUS
READERS.

NAVIGATOR

WWW.FOCUSREADERS.COM

Focus Readers is distributed by North Star Editions:
sales@northstareditions.com | 888-417-0195

Produced for Focus Readers by Red Line Editorial.

Content Consultant: Damien Caillaud, PhD, Assistant Professor of Anthropology, University of California, Davis

Photographs ©: Shutterstock Images, cover, 1, 4–5, 9 (top left), 9 (top right), 9 (bottom left), 9 (bottom right), 10–11, 13, 21, 22–23; iStockphoto, 7, 15, 16–17, 26; Antony Njuguna/Reuters/Newscom, 19; Red Line Editorial, 24; NHPA/Photoshot/Science Source, 29

Library of Congress Cataloging-in-Publication Data
Names: Bullard, Lisa, author.
Title: Saving mountain gorillas / by Lisa Bullard.
Description: Lake Elmo, MN : Focus Readers, [2021] | Series: Saving animals |
  Includes index. | Audience: Grades 4-6
Identifiers: LCCN 2020008869 (print) | LCCN 2020008870 (ebook) | ISBN
  9781644933886 (hardcover) | ISBN 9781644934647 (paperback) | ISBN
  9781644936160 (pdf) | ISBN 9781644935408 (ebook)
Subjects: LCSH: Mountain gorilla--Conservation--Juvenile literature.
Classification: LCC QL737.P94 B85 2021 (print) | LCC QL737.P94 (ebook) |
  DDC 599.884--dc23
LC record available at https://lccn.loc.gov/2020008869
LC ebook record available at https://lccn.loc.gov/2020008870

Printed in the United States of America
Mankato, MN
012021

ABOUT THE AUTHOR

Lisa Bullard is the author of more than 100 books for children, including the mystery novel *Turn Left at the Cow*. She also teaches writing classes for adults and children. Lisa grew up in Minnesota and now lives just north of Minneapolis.

TABLE OF CONTENTS

CHAPTER 1

MEALTIME ON THE MOUNTAIN

Mountain gorillas make their homes in high **cloud forests**. Temperatures there can fall below freezing. To stay warm, these great apes have thicker hair than other gorillas. Mountain gorillas live in only four national parks in Africa. These parks are in Central Africa and East Africa.

Male mountain gorillas can weigh 430 pounds (195 kg). Females can weigh 220 pounds (100 kg).

Most mountain gorillas live in family groups. An older male gorilla leads each group. This ape is known as the **dominant** silverback. The silverback protects his group. He also guides the group to food sources each day. The group includes several female gorillas and young gorillas.

EATING THEIR VEGGIES

Gorillas eat huge amounts of food to support their large bodies. Plants make up most of their diet. Their meals include bamboo shoots, thistles, and wild celery. Along with plants, they eat a small number of insects. A gorilla can eat more than 40 pounds (18 kg) of plants in one day.

Gorillas spend a lot of time eating. They take breaks to digest the food. The animals do **social grooming** with one another. Young gorillas play together. At night, gorillas shape plants into sleeping nests. The next day, the silverback finds a new place for the group to eat and rest.

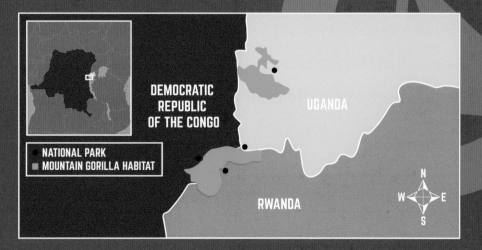

MOUNTAIN GORILLA RANGE

DEMOCRATIC REPUBLIC OF THE CONGO

UGANDA

RWANDA

● NATIONAL PARK
■ MOUNTAIN GORILLA HABITAT

N
W E
S

NOSEPRINTS

Scientists have closely studied mountain gorillas since the 1950s. They observe the gorillas in their forest homes. Some scientists have followed the same groups for many years at a time. George Schaller and Dian Fossey were two of the first scientists to do so.

At first, these scientists had trouble telling different gorillas apart. Then they made a discovery. They found that every mountain gorilla has a different set of nose wrinkles. These noseprints are as individual as human fingerprints. Schaller and Fossey made drawings and photos of individual gorillas' noseprints. That helped them track the behaviors of different gorillas.

Today, many scientists observe mountain gorillas in the wild. As part of their training, they

Mountain gorilla noses vary in their shapes, heights, widths, wrinkles, and more.

learn individual noseprints from photos. They also learn other unique parts of gorilla faces. But knowing one nose from another is still an important part of this work.

CHAPTER 2

GREAT GARDENERS

Mountain gorillas are important to plants. In fact, some people speak of these gorillas as gardeners. That's because mountain gorillas help plants grow. For example, mountain gorillas pull down branches to build nests. This creates openings for sunlight. The sunlight allows new plants to grow.

A mountain gorilla chews on a leaf in Uganda's Bwindi Impenetrable Forest.

Mountain gorillas also move through the forest. As they move, they leave dung behind. Dung is full of nutrients. These nutrients make the soil richer. They help new plants grow. The gorillas' dung also contains seeds. As a result, the dung plants seeds in new places.

Mountain gorillas eat large amounts of plants. Many of these plants grow quickly. Without gorillas, some plants might crowd out others. For this reason, mountain gorillas help maintain plant **biodiversity**. With less variety, other animals could be harmed. Certain animals might lose their sources of food and shelter. These animals might decrease in

Because cloud forests are found at high elevations, they are often covered by clouds.

number. Other animals might increase. Mountain gorillas help maintain the balance among these different animals. They help keep forests healthy.

The cloud forests are important to local people. The mountains receive large amounts of rain. The cloud forests help clean that rainwater. This clean water flows into nearby rivers and lakes.

People depend on this clean water for drinking, farming, and more. Without healthy forests, many people would lose their main water supplies.

In addition, cloud forests contain a huge variety of life. A number of plants

GORILLAS AND HUMANS

Gorillas are some of humans' closest relatives. They share several behaviors with people. For example, silverbacks form connections with their groups' young. Humans also form lasting bonds with children. These bonds last even after the children become adults. Most other mammals do not form these long-lasting connections. Learning why mountain gorillas are different helps scientists better understand humans.

Bamboo is the main source of food for golden monkeys.

and animals can only be found there.
Some examples include the golden
monkey and the African green broadbill.
These animals often do not receive as
much attention as mountain gorillas.
Fewer people are working to help them.
However, protecting gorilla homes helps
protect all other life-forms in those areas.

CHAPTER 3

IN DANGER

Mountain gorillas are large enough to be safe from most other animals. However, humans are putting gorillas at risk. A large number of people live near mountain gorillas. And these numbers keep increasing. In addition, Central Africa and East Africa have seen a great deal of conflict in recent decades.

Mountain gorilla mothers have few babies. The loss of any gorilla makes a difference.

Many people have been forced out of their homes. Some have moved to live near the gorillas.

Gorillas are at risk any time people get too close to them. The animals can catch human diseases. Gorillas can even die from diseases that aren't dangerous to people. Close contact with a human cold can put a whole group of gorillas at risk.

The large number of nearby people also leads to other problems for mountain gorillas. For example, people need food. So, they have been cutting down forest trees. Some create farms on the cleared land. Others use the wood to make **charcoal**. They use charcoal for cooking

A woman carries a load of charcoal in the Democratic Republic of the Congo.

fuel. When forests are cleared, gorillas lose areas where they can get food.

Many people in the region are poor. Some look for water in the forest. Others set traps there to catch antelopes to eat.

Gorillas can become trapped instead. Many of these actions are illegal. But people are trying to stay alive.

In other cases, military groups hide out in the forests. These groups sometimes kill gorillas. Rangers in the national parks

CLIMATE CHANGE

Climate change could cause more trouble for mountain gorillas. As weather patterns change, the plants that gorillas eat will change as well. Climate change may also bring more people into gorillas' territory. People will need to search for water and new land to grow food. They may push farther into the gorillas' mountain homes to find water and land. At some point, there may be nowhere left for gorillas to live.

A park ranger stands guard in the Democratic Republic of the Congo's Virunga National Park.

work hard to keep the gorillas safe. But the rangers are also at risk. Between 1999 and 2019, more than 175 rangers were killed. The area's conflicts continue to put both gorillas and people at risk.

CHAPTER 4

PROTECTING GORILLAS

Humans can be a danger to mountain gorillas. But many people are also working to help these animals. Some of these efforts have been successful. In 1989, experts estimated that only 620 mountain gorillas remained on Earth. In 2018, their numbers had increased to more than 1,000.

Some mountain gorilla groups have fewer than 10 members. Others contain more than 20.

Ecotourism is a big reason for this increase. Visitors pay to see mountain gorillas. This money supports national parks. It also supports the countries' economies. Rwanda, for instance, relies on the money made from tourism.

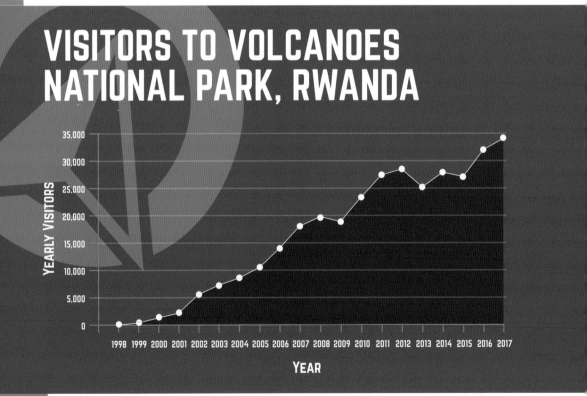

VISITORS TO VOLCANOES NATIONAL PARK, RWANDA

YEARLY VISITORS

35,000
30,000
25,000
20,000
15,000
10,000
5,000
0

1998 1999 2000 2001 2002 2003 2004 2005 2006 2007 2008 2009 2010 2011 2012 2013 2014 2015 2016 2017

YEAR

However, tourists can put mountain gorillas at risk. People can give gorillas diseases. For this reason, governments have taken steps to protect mountain gorillas. For example, visitors who appear to be ill are not allowed into the parks. Visitors also must stay at least 23 feet (7.0 m) away from the gorillas. In some parks, all visitors must wear face masks during tours.

But visitors can bring many benefits. They pay for places to stay. Taking care of visitors creates jobs. Visitors also buy local crafts. This money can make a difference. Local communities may feel that tourism improves their own lives.

A tourist poses for a photo near a mountain gorilla in Rwanda's Volcanoes National Park.

If locals believe this, they may work to protect mountain gorillas. People may also clear fewer trees in protected areas.

However, local people have received little of tourism's profits. Instead, most of the money ends up with people who do not live near the parks. Some money goes to governments and private companies. Other money goes to nonlocal people working for the parks.

As a result, local communities gain more from using the forests. So, they continue to put gorillas at risk. In 2005, Rwanda started sharing park income with local communities. But in 2017, few people knew about the program. And they still did not receive enough direct benefit. For these reasons, conflicts between people and gorillas remain.

At the same time, **conservation** groups are helping mountain gorillas. These groups study the best ways to help. They hire doctors who care for sick gorillas. They hire trackers who check on gorillas every day. The groups also make people around the world aware of the gorillas.

This attention can increase efforts to help mountain gorillas.

Groups have also helped local people. For example, groups have set up safe water sources for villages. They have found ways to cut down on the need for charcoal. These changes make people's lives better. They also reduce the need for people to enter gorillas' forests.

Governments are working to help mountain gorillas, too. In 2015, three countries signed an agreement. They agreed to work together to protect gorillas. The agreement helped scientists count the gorilla population in 2018. Gorilla numbers had increased. This

A park guard identifies a mountain gorilla to help track the gorilla population.

information helped show that current efforts might be working.

Many people understand why helping mountain gorillas matters. But the animals still face several dangers. People must continue working together to keep gorillas' numbers growing.

FOCUS ON
SAVING
MOUNTAIN GORILLAS

Write your answers on a separate piece of paper.

1. Write a paragraph about the key ideas of Chapter 2.

2. Do you think governments should make sure local people have a share in tourism's profits? Why or why not?

3. What kind of mountain gorilla leads its group?
   - **A.** silverback gorilla
   - **B.** mother gorilla
   - **C.** golden monkey

4. Why does keeping tourists a certain distance away from mountain gorillas help keep gorillas safe?
   - **A.** Tourists are less likely to scare mountain gorillas out of their homes.
   - **B.** Tourists are less likely to attack mountain gorillas.
   - **C.** Tourists are less likely to spread disease to mountain gorillas.

Answer key on page 32.

GLOSSARY

biodiversity
The number of different species that live in an area.

charcoal
A dark material made from wood that is used as fuel.

climate change
A human-caused global crisis involving long-term changes in Earth's temperature and weather patterns.

cloud forests
Forests at high elevations that receive large amounts of mist and rain.

conservation
The careful protection of plants, animals, and natural resources so they are not lost or wasted.

dominant
Having more power or getting first choice of resources such as food, water, or mates.

ecotourism
The activity of visiting natural areas with a focus on conserving those places.

social grooming
An activity that involves cleaning the fur and skin of another animal.

TO LEARN MORE

BOOKS

Daly, Ruth. *Bringing Back the Mountain Gorilla*. New York: Crabtree Publishing, 2020.

Machajewski, Sarah. *The Return of the Mountain Gorilla*. New York: PowerKids Press, 2018.

Nippert-Eng, Christena. *Gorillas Up Close*. New York: Henry Holt, 2016.

NOTE TO EDUCATORS

Visit **www.focusreaders.com** to find lesson plans, activities, links, and other resources related to this title.

INDEX

Answer Key: 1. Answers will vary; **2.** Answers will vary; **3.** A; **4.** C